Contents

Questions

1) Can you name all 13 teams that have played in the IPL?

2) Who bowled the first ever ball in the IPL?

3) Who scored the first ever IPL hundred?

4) Which team won the first ever IPL title?

5) Who claimed the first ever IPL hat-trick for the Chennai Super Kings against Kings XI Punjab in 2008?

6) In which year was TV decision review system first used in the IPL?

7) Which two sides competed in the first super over in the IPL?

8) Mumbai Indians' Harbhajan Singh was banned for the remainder of the 2008 IPL after slapping which Kings XI player after the match between the two sides?

9) Which country was the 2009 IPL held in?

10) Which team had to play two super overs in the space of ten days after tying games against Sunrisers Hyderabad and Delhi Daredevils?

11) Kings XI beat Deccan Chargers by 1 run in 2009, which Kings XI bowler returned figures of 3 wickets for 13 runs off his 4 overs?

12) Chennai won the opening match of the 2011 IPL by two runs against which team?

13) Chris Gayle broke the record for the highest individual IPL score when he scored how many runs against Pune Warriors in 2013?

14) In that innings Gayle hit the fastest IPL hundred by reaching three figures in how many deliveries?

15) How many sixes did Gayle hit in that innings?

16) Gayle also bowled one over in the match, how many wickets did he take?

17) Kings XI Punjab beat which team by two runs in the group stage in 2012?

18) Which team did Sachin Tendulkar represent throughout his IPL career?

19) In which year did Virat Kohli make his IPL debut for RCB?

20) Who was head coach of the Kolkata Knight Riders when they won the IPL in 2012 and 2014?

21) Who became head coach of CSK in 2009 after playing for them in the 2008 season?

22) Which player broke the record for the most expensive overseas signing ahead of the 2020 season?

23) Who was the most expensive overseas player in the first ever IPL auction?

24) Which bowler took 32 wickets during the 2013 IPL season?

25) Who took the most wickets in the first IPL season in 2008 by claiming 22 victims?

26) Who was the leading bowler with 28 wickets in the 2011 season?

27) Virat Kohli scored an incredible 973 runs in the 2016 season, but how many hundreds did he score in the season?

28) Which player scored nine 50's in the 2016 season without scoring any hundreds?

29) Which Australian scored 733 runs in the 2013 season?

30) Who won the man of the match award in the first ever IPL final after taking three wickets and scoring a half century?

31) Who took four wickets in the 2009 final and won the man of the match award despite finishing on the losing side?

32) Who won the man of the tournament award for the first season of the IPL?

33) Sunil Narine won his first man of the tournament award in what year?

34) Rohit Sharma won the award for being the best young player of the tournament in which year?

35) Who won the emerging player of the year award in 2014?

36) Jofra Archer claimed three wickets on his IPL debut in 2018 versus which team?

37) Who did Jasprit Bumrah dismiss to claim his first ever IPL wicket?

38) Who took a great catch to dismiss Vinay Kumar in the penultimate over of the 2009 final?

39) Which fielder produced two run outs in the 20th over as the Mumbai Indians were dismissed, leading to a super over in the match with Gujarat Lions in 2017?

40) Trent Boult took a stunning one-handed catch on the boundary to dismiss which RCB player in April 2018?

41) Who recorded the worst ever bowling figures in the IPL when he was hit for 70 runs off his four overs versus RCB in 2018?

42) Ishant Sharma was smashed for 66 runs in his four overs by which team in 2013?

43) Spinner Mujeeb Ur Rahman conceded 66 runs against which team in 2019?

44) Who scored 99 as Delhi Capitals tied with KKR in 2019, before Delhi went on to win the super over?

45) In which stadium was the first match of the IPL played in 2014?

46) Which non-wicketkeeper was the first to reach 100 career catches in the IPL?

47) Which player took four catches for the Chennai Super Kings in a match versus KKR in 2019?

48) Rajasthan Royals lost by one run to which team in the 2012 group stage?

49) Pune Warriors lost by one run despite only chasing 121 for victory against which side in 2012?

50) In which year did the Mumbai Indians win their first IPL title?

51) Sunrisers Hyderabad beat which team in the 2016 IPL final?

52) Which West Indian took figures of 6 wickets for 12 runs for the Mumbai Indians against Sunrisers Hyderabad in 2019?

53) Anil Kumble took a sensational 5 for 5 against which team whilst playing for RCB in 2009?

54) Which South African took a hat-trick for CSK against KKR in 2008?

55) Who scored his first IPL hundred for Rising Pune Supergiant against Gujarat Lions in 2017?

56) Who hit a match winning 83 off 30 balls as stand-in captain for the Mumbai Indians as they beat Kings XI Punjab off the last ball in 2019?

57) When Royal Challengers Bangalore were bowled our for 49 by the Kolkata Knight Riders in 2017, which New Zealander took 3 wickets for 4 runs?

58) Kings XI Punjab struggled to 92/8 off 20 overs against the Chennai Super Kings in 2009, which bowler took 2 wickets for 8 runs off his 4 overs?

59) Which player smashed 52 sixes during the 2019 season?

60) In October 2019 it was announced that who would become head coach of Kings XI Punjab?

61) Who did Virat Kohli replace as RCB captain in 2013?

62) Which team did Shane Warne captain throughout his IPL career?

63) Stuart Broad played two season of IPL cricket for which team?

64) Andre Russell began his IPL career in 2012 playing for who?

65) Who became the first Nepalese player in IPL history in 2018?

66) Which South African bowler took 25 wickets, more than anybody else, in the 2012 season?

67) Andrew Tye was the leading wicket taker in which IPL season?

68) Which Australian toped the run scoring charts in the first IPL season in 2008?

69) In which year did Sachin Tendulkar top the run scoring charts with 618 runs?

70) Which Australian won the Most Valuable Player award in 2014?

71) Who scored 89 runs in the 2012 final to secure the man of the match award?

72) Which Bangladesh player won the emerging player of the year award in 2016?

73) Which Australian went for 61 off his four overs in a match between RCB and the Sunrisers in 2016?

74) Spinner Imran Tahir bowled four overs and conceded 59 runs whilst playing for the Delhi Daredevils against which team in 2016?

75) In 2014 Rajasthan and KKR tied after twenty overs and then both hit 11 runs in the super over, why were Rajasthan declared the winners?

76) Which player was only a few metres away from hitting a match winning six for the Delhi Daredevils against CSK in 2015, finishing on 73 not out?

77) Mumbai Indians won the 2019 title in dramatic fashion by one run when Lasith Malinga dismissed which CSK batsman with the last ball of the game?

78) MS Dhoni was run out in the 2019 final by which player?

79) Who became the first person to take three IPL hat-tricks in their career?

80) Who hit 122 of 58 balls in the second qualifier in 2014 to send Kings XI Punjab to the final?

81) Kevin Pietersen hit his only IPL hundred for the Delhi Daredevils against Deccan Chargers in what year?

82) Who won the emerging player of the year award for the 2019 season?

83) Who was the leading run scorer in both 2011 and 2012?

84) Which player topped the wicket taking charts in both 2016 and 2017?

85) Which Australian won the man of the match in the 2016 final?

86) Which Englishman won the MVP award in 2017?

87) Which Australian was captain of Kings XI Punjab in 2014 and 2015?

88) Which New Zealander captained Pune Warriors India for one game in 2013?

89) Who was head coach of Deccan Chargers as they won the 2009 IPL?

90) Who hit an astonishing 59 sixes during the 2012 season?

91) Which team bowled the Rajasthan Royals out for 58 runs in 2009?

92) Which team was bowled out for under 70 runs twice in the space of two weeks in 2017?

93) Which Englishman scored a century during the 2019 season?

94) Who hit 113 off 58 balls as Chennai Super Kings won the second qualifier in 2012 to secure their place in the final?

95) CSK beat Kings XI by 10 wickets in April 2013 thanks to unbeaten half centuries from which two players?

96) Mumbai Indians won the second qualifier in 2013 to gain a place in the final after which player hit a four off the fifth ball of the twentieth over to knock out the Rajasthan Royals?

97) Kings XI chased down 206 with an over to spare against Chennai in April 2014 thanks, in part, to which player hitting 95 off 43 balls?

98) Who became the first batsman to reach 5000 runs in the IPL?

99) Which two players hold the record for an opening partnership in the IPL with a stand of 185 runs?

100) AB de Villiers took a brilliant jumping catch on the boundary edge to catch which Sunrisers batsman in 2018?

101) Which bowler took two hat-tricks in the 2009 season?

102) Chennai were restricted to 125/9 in chasing 149 in the 2013 final, despite which player hitting an unbeaten 63?

103) Who hit a boundary in the last over to seal the title for Kolkata Knight Riders in 2014?

104) Who was the only man to reach double figures as RCB were dismissed for 70 by CSK in March 2019?

105) Which wicket-keeper/batsman struck the most sixes during the 2009 campaign?

106) Quinton De Kock began his IPL career with which side?

107) Sanath Jayasuriya played in the first three years of the IPL for which team?

108) Which Australian was bought by Mumbai Indians for $1,000,000 in 2013?

109) Which Englishman was the most expensive player in both the 2017 and 2018 auctions?

110) Who was the leading wicket taker during the 2019 campaign?

111) Who scored the most runs in the 2019 IPL?

112) Who won the MVP award for the 2016 IPL season?

113) Which bowler won the man of the match award in the 2019 final?

114) Which wicket keeper/batsman won the emerging player of the year award in 2018?

115) Which Indian captained Kochi Tuskers Kerala on one occasion during his career?

116) Which team has Afghanistan's Mujeeb Ur Rahman represented throughout his IPL career?

117) Who became the first man to reach 100 IPL wickets in 2013?

118) Mumbai Indians beat which team by 146 runs in May 2017?

119) Who hit a brilliant 128 not out off 63 balls for the Daredevils against Sunrisers Hyderabad in 2018?

120) Who was Steve Smith playing for when he hit his maiden IPL hundred?

121) Which Englishman took a hat-trick during the 2019 edition of the IPL?

122) Adam Gilchrist decided to have a bowl in his final ever appearance and unbelievably dismissed which player with his first delivery?

123) Kieron Pollard caught which CSK batsman with an acrobatic one-handed effort in 2019?

124) Which player won the IPL catch of the season award in both 2016 and 2017?

125) Which players put together a record partnership of 229 in 2016?

126) Which team conceded 28 extras in a match against KKR to break the IPL record in 2008?

127) Who hit a quick-fire 38 runs off 9 balls versus Rising Pune Supergiant in 2017?

128) Who hit a last ball boundary to seal a victory for Rajasthan over Sunrisers Hyderabad in 2015?

129) Who hit 82 not out off 32 balls in a losing cause, as Delhi fell one run short against the Gujarat Lions in 2016?

130) Who bowled the crucial final over as Mumbai beat Rising Pune Supergiant by one run in the 2017 final?

131) Which Englishman hit 56 off 23 balls to help Chennai to a last over group stage win over Kolkata in 2018?

132) How many IPL hundreds did Chris Gayle make?

133) AB de Villiers scored his maiden IPL hundred whilst playing for which team?

134) Which team hammered RCB by 118 runs in 2019?

135) The Delhi Daredevils scored only 80 runs despite batting for 19.1 overs against which team in 2013?

136) Chris Gayle hit more sixes than anybody else in how many IPL seasons?

137) Daniel Vettori was head coach of which team from 2014 to 2018?

138) Justin Langer spent two seasons playing for which IPL franchise?

139) Who did Andrew Flintoff play for in his one IPL season in 2009?

140) By the end of the 2019 season which player had the most scores of 50 or more in IPL history with 48?

141) In 2014 who became the first Indian player to take 100 wickets in the IPL?

142) In a match between CSK and Mumbai in 2013, Kieron Pollard incredibly dropped which batsman three times off three successive deliveries?

143) Which two Australians put on 206 for the 2nd wicket for Kings XI against RCB in 2011?

144) Which New Zealand player hit a four off the last ball of the game to guide Rajasthan Royals to a win over Delhi in April 2015?

145) MS Dhoni hit a four and three sixes off the last over to guide Rising Pune Supergiant to a memorable win against Kings XI Punjab in 2016, but which bowler was on the receiving end of the Dhoni masterclass?

146) Which Englishman guided Delhi to a last-ball win over Mumbai in 2018 with an innings of 91 not out off 53 balls?

147) Mumbai beat which team by 102 runs in May 2018?

148) Who was the first man from Holland to play in the IPL in 2011?

149) Shane Bond played his only IPL season in 2010 for which team?

150) KKR sensationally chased 183 against Gujarat Lions in 2017 without losing a wicket, which two batsmen were not out?

151) Who became the first player to register 100 IPL wins as captain?

Answers

1) Can you name all 13 teams that have played in the IPL?

Chennai Super Kings
Deccan Chargers
Delhi Daredevils/Capitals
Gujarat Lions
Kings XI Punjab
Kochi Tuskers Kerala
Kolkata Knight Riders
Mumbai Indians
Pune Warriors India
Rajasthan Royals
Rising Pune Supergiant
Royal Challengers Bangalore
Sunrisers Hyderabad

2) Who bowled the first ever ball in the IPL?
Praveen Kumar

3) Who scored the first ever IPL hundred?
Brendon McCullum

4) Which team won the first ever IPL title?
Rajasthan Royals

5) Who claimed the first ever IPL hat-trick for the Chennai Super Kings against Kings XI Punjab in 2008?
Lakshmipathy Balaji

6) In which year was TV decision review system first used in the IPL?
2018

7) Which two sides competed in the first super over in the IPL?
Rajasthan Royals and KKR (The Royals won)

8) Mumbai Indians' Harbhajan Singh was banned for the remainder of the 2008 IPL after slapping which Kings XI player after the match between the two sides?
Sreesanth

9) Which country was the 2009 IPL held in?
South Africa

10) Which team had to play two super overs in the space of ten days after tying games against Sunrisers Hyderabad and Delhi Daredevils?
Royal Challengers Bangalore

11) Kings XI beat Deccan Chargers by 1 run in 2009, which Kings XI bowler returned figures of 3 wickets for 13 runs off his 4 overs?
Yuvraj Singh

12) Chennai won the opening match of the 2011 IPL by two runs against which team?
KKR

13) Chris Gayle broke the record for the highest individual IPL score when he scored how many runs against Pune Warriors in 2013?
175 not out

14) In that innings Gayle hit the fastest IPL hundred by reaching three figures in how many deliveries?

30

15) How many sixes did Gayle hit in that innings?

17

16) Gayle also bowled one over in the match, how many wickets did he take?

Two

17) Kings XI Punjab beat which team by two runs in the group stage in 2012?

KKR

18) Which team did Sachin Tendulkar represent throughout his IPL career?

Mumbai Indians

19) In which year did Virat Kohli make his IPL debut for RCB?

2008

20) Who was head coach of the Kolkata Knight Riders when they won the IPL in 2012 and 2014?
Trevor Bayliss

21) Who became head coach of CSK in 2009 after playing for them in the 2008 season?
Stephen Fleming

22) Which player broke the record for the most expensive overseas signing ahead of the 2020 season?
Pat Cummins

23) Who was the most expensive overseas player in the first ever IPL auction?
Andrew Symonds

24) Which bowler took 32 wickets during the 2013 IPL season?
Dwayne Bravo

25) Who took the most wickets in the first IPL season in 2008 by claiming 22 victims?

Sohail Tanvir

26) Who was the leading bowler with 28 wickets in the 2011 season?

Lasith Malinga

27) Virat Kohli scored an incredible 973 runs in the 2016 season, but how many hundreds did he score in the season?

Four

28) Which player scored nine 50's in the 2016 season without scoring any hundreds?

David Warner

29) Which Australian scored 733 runs in the 2013 season?

Michael Hussey

30) Who won the man of the match award in the first ever IPL final after taking three wickets and scoring a half century?
Yusuf Pathan

31) Who took four wickets in the 2009 final and won the man of the match award despite finishing on the losing side?
Anil Kumble

32) Who won the man of the tournament award for the first season of the IPL?
Shane Watson

33) Sunil Narine won his first man of the tournament award in what year?
2012

34) Rohit Sharma won the award for being the best young player of the tournament in which year?
2009

35) Who won the emerging player of the year award in 2014?

Axar Patel

36) Jofra Archer claimed three wickets on his IPL debut in 2018 versus which team?

Mumbai Indians

37) Who did Jasprit Bumrah dismiss to claim his first ever IPL wicket?

Virat Kohli

38) Who took a great catch to dismiss Vinay Kumar in the penultimate over of the 2009 final?

Harmeet Singh

39) Which fielder produced two run outs in the 20th over as the Mumbai Indians were dismissed, leading to a super over in the match with Gujarat Lions in 2017?

Ravindra Jadeja

40) Trent Boult took a stunning one-handed catch on the boundary to dismiss which RCB player in April 2018?
Virat Kohli

41) Who recorded the worst ever bowling figures in the IPL when he was hit for 70 runs off his four overs versus RCB in 2018?
Basil Thampi

42) Ishant Sharma was smashed for 66 runs in his four overs by which team in 2013?
CSK

43) Spinner Mujeeb Ur Rahman conceded 66 runs against which team in 2019?
Sunrisers Hyderabad

44) Who scored 99 as Delhi Capitals tied with KKR in 2019, before Delhi went on to win the super over?
Prithvi Shaw

45) In which stadium was the first match of
the IPL played in 2014?
Sheikh Zayed Stadium in Abu Dhabi

46) Which non-wicketkeeper was the first to
reach 100 career catches in the IPL?
Suresh Raina

47) Which player took four catches for the
Chennai Super Kings in a match versus
KKR in 2019?
Faf du Plessis

48) Rajasthan Royals lost by one run to
which team in the 2012 group stage?
Delhi Daredevils

49) Pune Warriors lost by one run despite
only chasing 121 for victory against
which side in 2012?
Mumbai Indians

50) In which year did the Mumbai Indians
win their first IPL title?
2013

51) Sunrisers Hyderabad beat which team in the 2016 IPL final?
Royal Challengers Bangalore

52) Which West Indian took figures of 6 wickets for 12 runs for the Mumbai Indians against Sunrisers Hyderabad in 2019?
Alzarri Joseph

53) Anil Kumble took a sensational 5 for 5 against which team whilst playing for RCB in 2009?
Rajasthan Royals

54) Which South African took a hat-trick for CSK against KKR in 2008?
Makhaya Ntini

55) Who scored his first IPL hundred for Rising Pune Supergiant against Gujarat Lions in 2017?
Ben Stokes

56) Who hit a match winning 83 off 30 balls as stand-in captain for the Mumbai Indians as they beat Kings XI Punjab off the last ball in 2019?
Kieron Pollard

57) When Royal Challengers Bangalore were bowled our for 49 by the Kolkata Knight Riders in 2017, which New Zealander took 3 wickets for 4 runs?
Colin de Grandhomme

58) Kings XI Punjab struggled to 92/8 off 20 overs against the Chennai Super Kings in 2009, which bowler took 2 wickets for 8 runs off his 4 overs?
Muttiah Muralitharan

59) Which player smashed 52 sixes during the 2019 season?
Andre Russell

60) In October 2019 it was announced that who would become head coach of Kings XI Punjab?
Anil Kumble

61) Who did Virat Kohli replace as RCB captain in 2013?
Daniel Vettori

62) Which team did Shane Warne captain throughout his IPL career?
Rajasthan Royals

63) Stuart Broad played two season of IPL cricket for which team?
Kings XI Punjab

64) Andre Russell began his IPL career in 2012 playing for who?
Delhi Daredevils

65) Who became the first Nepalese player in IPL history in 2018?
Sandeep Lamichhane

66) Which South African bowler took 25
wickets, more than anybody else, in the
2012 season?
Morne Morkel

67) Andrew Tye was the leading wicket
taker in which IPL season?
2018

68) Which Australian toped the run scoring
charts in the first IPL season in 2008?
Shaun Marsh

69) In which year did Sachin Tendulkar top
the run scoring charts with 618 runs?
2010

70) Which Australian won the Most
Valuable Player award in 2014?
Glenn Maxwell

71) Who scored 89 runs in the 2012 final to
secure the man of the match award?
Manvinder Bisla

72) Which Bangladesh player won the emerging player of the year award in 2016?
Mustafizur Rahman

73) Which Australian went for 61 off his four overs in a match between RCB and the Sunrisers in 2016?
Shane Watson

74) Spinner Imran Tahir bowled four overs and conceded 59 runs whilst playing for the Delhi Daredevils against which team in 2016?
Mumbai Indians

75) In 2014 Rajasthan and KKR tied after twenty overs and then both hit 11 runs in the super over, why were Rajasthan declared the winners?
They hit more boundaries

76) Which player was only a few metres away from hitting a match winning six for the Delhi Daredevils against CSK in 2015, finishing on 73 not out?
Albie Morkel

77) Mumbai Indians won the 2019 title in dramatic fashion by one run when Lasith Malinga dismissed which CSK batsman with the last ball of the game?
Shardul Thakur

78) MS Dhoni was run out in the 2019 final by which player?
Ishan Kishan

79) Who became the first person to take three IPL hat-tricks in their career?
Amit Mishra

80) Who hit 122 of 58 balls in the second qualifier in 2014 to send Kings XI Punjab to the final?
Virender Sehwag

81) Kevin Pietersen hit his only IPL hundred
for the Delhi Daredevils against Deccan
Chargers in what year?
2012

82) Who won the emerging player of the
year award for the 2019 season?
Shubman Gill

83) Who was the leading run scorer in both
2011 and 2012?
Chris Gayle

84) Which player topped the wicket taking
charts in both 2016 and 2017?
Bhuvneshwar Kumar

85) Which Australian won the man of the
match in the 2016 final?
Ben Cutting

86) Which Englishman won the MVP award
in 2017?
Ben Stokes

87) Which Australian was captain of Kings XI Punjab in 2014 and 2015?

George Bailey

88) Which New Zealander captained Pune Warriors India for one game in 2013?

Ross Taylor

89) Who was head coach of Deccan Chargers as they won the 2009 IPL?

Darren Lehmann

90) Who hit an astonishing 59 sixes during the 2012 season?

Chris Gayle

91) Which team bowled the Rajasthan Royals out for 58 runs in 2009?

RCB

92) Which team was bowled out for under 70 runs twice in the space of two weeks in 2017?

Delhi Capitals

93) Which Englishman scored a century
during the 2019 season?
Jonny Bairstow

94) Who hit 113 off 58 balls as Chennai
Super Kings won the second qualifier in
2012 to secure their place in the final?
Murali Vijay

95) CSK beat Kings XI by 10 wickets in April
2013 thanks to unbeaten half centuries
from which two players?
Murali Vijay and Michael Hussey

96) Mumbai Indians won the second
qualifier in 2013 to gain a place in the
final after which player hit a four off the
fifth ball of the twentieth over to knock
out the Rajasthan Royals?
Harbhajan Singh

97) Kings XI chased down 206 with an over to spare against Chennai in April 2014 thanks, in part, to which player hitting 95 off 43 balls?
Glenn Maxwell

98) Who became the first batsman to reach 5000 runs in the IPL?
Suresh Raina

99) Which two players hold the record for an opening partnership in the IPL with a stand of 185 runs?
Jonny Bairstow and David Warner

100) AB de Villiers took a brilliant jumping catch on the boundary edge to catch which Sunrisers batsman in 2018?
Alex Hales

101) Which bowler took two hat-tricks in the 2009 season?
Yuvraj Singh

102) Chennai were restricted to 125/9 in chasing 149 in the 2013 final, despite which player hitting an unbeaten 63?
MS Dhoni

103) Who hit a boundary in the last over to seal the title for Kolkata Knight Riders in 2014?
Piyush Chawla

104) Who was the only man to reach double figures as RCB were dismissed for 70 by CSK in March 2019?
Parthiv Patel

105) Which wicket-keeper/batsman struck the most sixes during the 2009 campaign?
Adam Gilchrist

106) Quinton De Kock began his IPL career with which side?
Sunrisers Hyderabad

107) Sanath Jayasuriya played in the first
three years of the IPL for which team?
Mumbai Indians

108) Which Australian was bought by
Mumbai Indians for $1,000,000 in 2013?
Glenn Maxwell

109) Which Englishman was the most
expensive player in both the 2017 and
2018 auctions?
Ben Stokes

110) Who was the leading wicket taker
during the 2019 campaign?
Imran Tahir

111) Who scored the most runs in the 2019
IPL?
David Warner

112) Who won the MVP award for the 2016
IPL season?
Virat Kohli

113) Which bowler won the man of the match award in the 2019 final?

Jasprit Bumrah

114) Which wicket keeper/batsman won the emerging player of the year award in 2018?

Rishabh Pant

115) Which Indian captained Kochi Tuskers Kerala on one occasion during his career?

Parthiv Patel

116) Which team has Afghanistan's Mujeeb Ur Rahman represented throughout his IPL career?

Kings XI Punjab

117) Who became the first man to reach 100 IPL wickets in 2013?

Lasith Malinga

118) Mumbai Indians beat which team by 146 runs in May 2017?
Delhi Daredevils

119) Who hit a brilliant 128 not out off 63 balls for the Daredevils against Sunrisers Hyderabad in 2018?
Rishabh Pant

120) Who was Steve Smith playing for when he hit his maiden IPL hundred?
Rise Pune Supergiant

121) Which Englishman took a hat-trick during the 2019 edition of the IPL?
Sam Curran

122) Adam Gilchrist decided to have a bowl in his final ever appearance and unbelievably dismissed which player with his first delivery?
Harbhajan Singh

123) Kieron Pollard caught which CSK batsman with an acrobatic one-handed effort in 2019?
Suresh Raina

124) Which player won the IPL catch of the season award in both 2016 and 2017?
Suresh Raina

125) Which players put together a record partnership of 229 in 2016?
Virat Kohli and AB de Villiers

126) Which team conceded 28 extras in a match against KKR to break the IPL record in 2008?
Deccan Chargers

127) Who hit a quick-fire 38 runs off 9 balls versus Rising Pune Supergiant in 2017?
Chris Morris

128) Who hit a last ball boundary to seal a victory for Rajasthan over Sunrisers Hyderabad in 2015?

James Faulkner

129) Who hit 82 not out off 32 balls in a losing cause, as Delhi fell one run short against the Gujarat Lions in 2016?
Chris Morris

130) Who bowled the crucial final over as Mumbai beat Rising Pune Supergiant by one run in the 2017 final?
Mitchell Johnson

131) Which Englishman hit 56 off 23 balls to help Chennai to a last over group stage win over Kolkata in 2018?
Sam Billings

132) How many IPL hundreds did Chris Gayle make?
Six

133) AB de Villiers scored his maiden IPL hundred whilst playing for which team?
Delhi Daredevils

134) Which team hammered RCB by 118 runs in 2019?
Sunrisers Hyderabad

135) The Delhi Daredevils scored only 80 runs despite batting for 19.1 overs against which team in 2013?
Sunrisers Hyderabad

136) Chris Gayle hit more sixes than anybody else in how many IPL seasons?
Five

137) Daniel Vettori was head coach of which team from 2014 to 2018?
RCB

138) Justin Langer spent two seasons playing for which IPL franchise?
Rajasthan Royals

139) Who did Andrew Flintoff play for in his one IPL season in 2009?
CSK

140) By the end of the 2019 season which player had the most scores of 50 or more in IPL history with 48?
David Warner

141) In 2014 who became the first Indian player to take 100 wickets in the IPL?
Amit Mishra

142) In a match between CSK and Mumbai in 2013, Kieron Pollard incredibly dropped which batsman three times off three successive deliveries?
Michael Hussey

143) Which two Australians put on 206 for the 2nd wicket for Kings XI against RCB in 2011?
Adam Gilchrist and Shaun Marsh

144) Which New Zealand player hit a four off the last ball of the game to guide Rajasthan Royals to a win over Delhi in April 2015?
Tim Southee

145) MS Dhoni hit a four and three sixes off the last over to guide Rising Pune Supergiant to a memorable win against Kings XI Punjab in 2016, but which bowler was on the receiving end of the Dhoni masterclass?

Axar Patel

146) Which Englishman guided Delhi to a last-ball win over Mumbai in 2018 with an innings of 91 not out off 53 balls?

Jason Roy

147) Mumbai beat which team by 102 runs in May 2018?

KKR

148) Who was the first man from Holland to play in the IPL in 2011?

Ryan ten Doeschate

149) Shane Bond played his only IPL season in 2010 for which team?

Kolkata Knight Riders

150) KKR sensationally chased 183 against Gujarat Lions in 2017 without losing a wicket, which two batsmen were not out?
Chris Lynn and Gautam Gambhir

151) Who became the first player to register 100 IPL wins as captain?
MS Dhoni

Printed in Great Britain
by Amazon